Mon Treal

By RL Lane

Mon Treal. Mon means "my". I remember that from French class…

Treal.

Trio?

Three? No.

What does it mean? Treal.

Does everything have to mean something?

Or can it just simply mean…

Montreal…

Montreal

By RL Lane

Air port? Newark airport. The port for air?

Will anyone go? I do not think they have fresh air…

I had drawn the plane and the terrain while I was in the clouds…

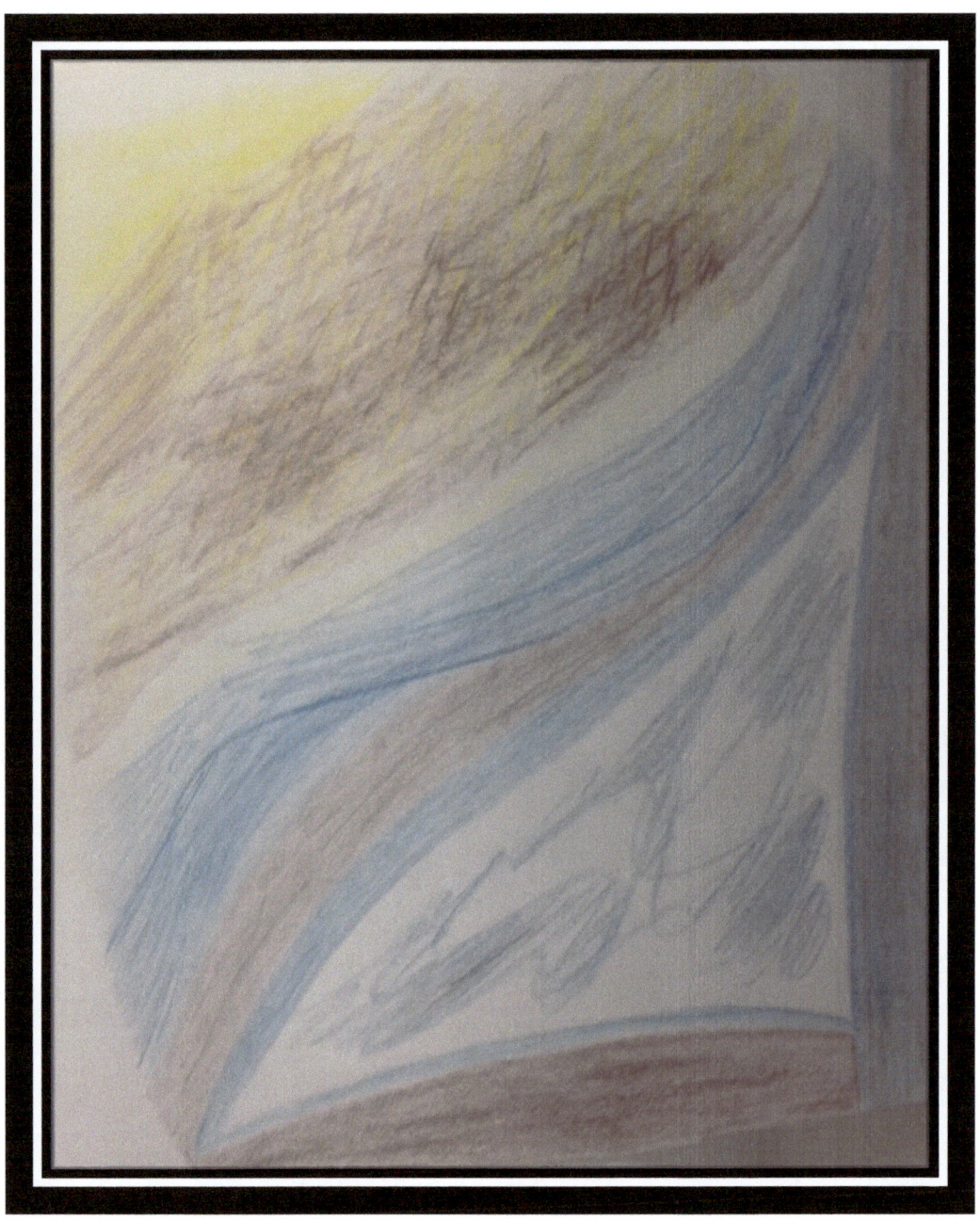

I landed. Zi French! Zi French! I walked out of Thad…the Montreal airport to catch my taxi and saw the orange lillies. Hi Mom! My Mom loved her orange Lillie's…lillies. I remembered there is French-Canadian on my Mom's side. Who are Thad and Lillie?

Montreal is part of the province of Quebec. My feet were soon walking upon their sidewalks. I looked down. My feet were the same…

Only the sidewalks had changed. So why did I feel different?

My same feet walked along. The only thing that had changed was the sidewalks, so why did I feel different?

I couldn't decide which paragraph about walking I liked best, so I left them both.

I met a lot of people while I was there. Oliver from the cab ride told me it was a city of discrimination. You can't get a job here unless you are from here he had said. I wasn't looking for a job, so I wasn't that concerned if he was right or wrong. I asked him what all the buildings with crosses were. It was a silly question. Of course they were churches. I was surprised how many there were. Oliver says there are so many churches. Beautiful historic ones that no one goes to. He said only the old go there. He says they have nothing else to do. Can someone tell the Pope. Montreal has lost its faith…

The city ozone…the city is one of the most bilingual in Quebec. The people from France say the Montreal French language is its own thing. An old French like Old Montreal. I had been there before. Old Montreal. One rainy day. Running over the cobblestone in and out of the little shops with my daughter. It is actually one of my favorite memories…

Ozine? Ozone. It is a pale blue gas with a distinctively pungent smell.

Ozine? There is no ozine, but there is an Ozine Fest. It is an annual anime convention organized by the editorial committee of Otakuzine Anime Magazine, a local magazine published in the Philippines. The event features a variety of activities including art contests. *I would like to win an art contest one day…*

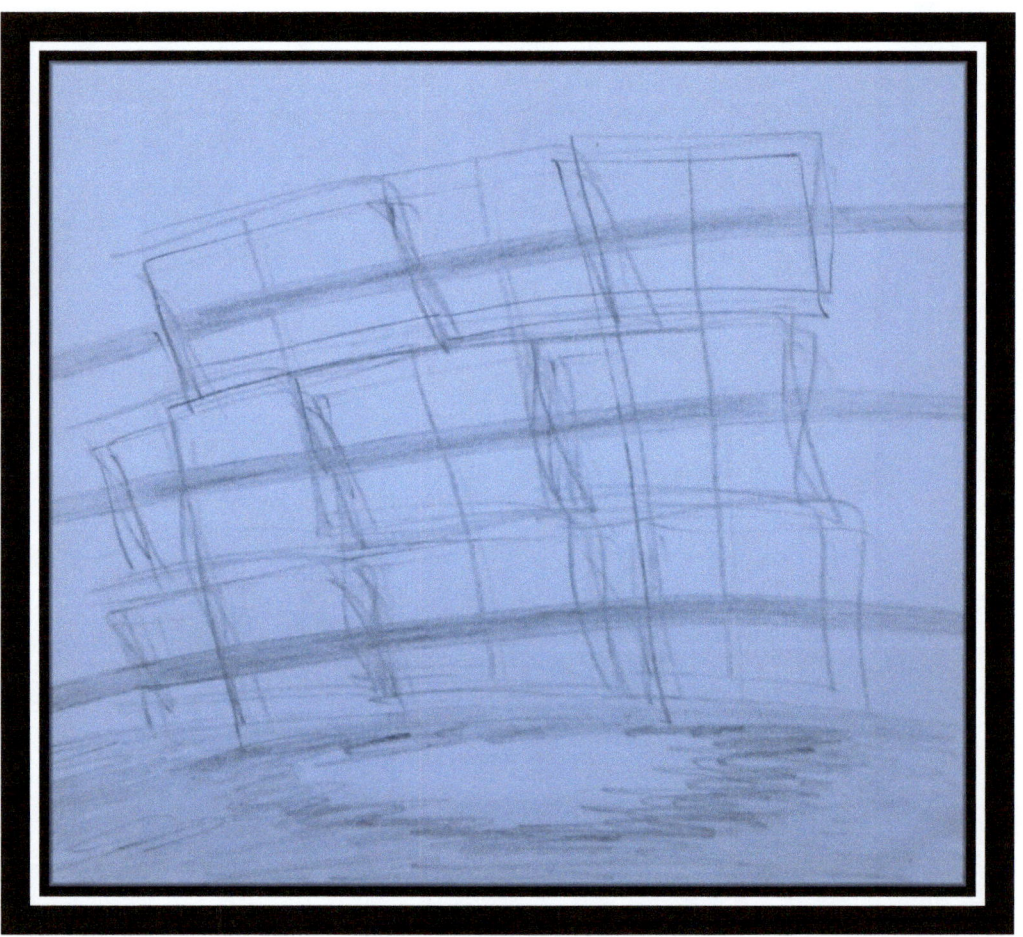

I was here this time for work. I spent the day with people much different than I. Some who wanted to pretend they were of the same echelon as the customers they serviced. Some who didn't care they had no money. Some young. Some older.

The women of the city were all beautifully dressed. A lot of colors. Their streets had flowers. It was the summertime…

I had a dream about a Tracy before I came to Montreal. I had seen her shortly after the message of Lisa XXXXXX in "Johnni and Georg". I met a Tracy on my trip. At first I thought it was her, but then I realized it was not. I guess we will meet her in the future. It is odd seeing people before you meet them. Why her I keep wondering…

The food and desserts of Montreal were fabulous. Crepes and Croissants. Oh. It should be a poem…

Crepes of crepe paper

Is that what we used to make those pretty flowers?

Croissants of all flavors

Flaky and light

I didn't see any flaky people

They all seemed smart

They seemed like they had purposes

Except for the one on his crate

Many of them rode their bikes

In the designated lanes

They seemed fairly happy

As they went about their day…

They greet each other with kisses. I wonder if they have more germs than the US. We do not kiss. We can barely touch. They laugh too, I noticed. They talk too. A lot. Always talking. The chatter everywhere.

Someone said she would be leaving Canada one day. They started talking about Quebec and how it still wanted to be its own thing. Some scare of that actually happening caused a lot of businesses to move to Toronto. The changes that would ensue if they were their own country had caused the organized companies to migrate away. Were they afraid to stand alone? Had they been a part of something for too long and could not see themselves alone ever again? It actually made me think of marriages. The ones together for so many years. The people who stay married long after they should because they too are afraid to be alone ever again. I can understand. It is nice to appear together. Society likes us together. Many of us like together. I liked the idea of together. Unfortunately, I was never really "together".

This book is not about bad relationships. It is supposed to be about this city I love. It did actually just occur to me what the message is, but we are not at the end, so we have to keep typing...

I stopped in a small convenience store to get a drink. I didn't see him on the way in. I sat at an outdoor table and saw him there a few minutes later. He was sitting on a crate, smoking his cigarette, with the cup in his hand outstretched. It seemed empty. I watched him for a long time. He smoked his cigarette to the very end. He did not look that dirty. His shoes, his clothes were too clean and new looking for me to believe he was homeless. The cap on his head was new. He was wearing glasses. He was an older gentleman. He had the routine down. Every squeak of the convenient store door stirred him to responsiveness, the cup in his hand motioning toward a person. He would greet everyone going by. It seemed Montreal should pay him for his greeting services. I wondered why he was there. It saddened me to see that this was how he was spending his time.

That last amount of time in the latter phase of a life. On a hot summer sidewalk. He did have a newspaper to read. He was reading it in between squeaks of the door. I doubt he was looking for a job. He seemed fairly content. He seemed certainly less stressed than I was just watching him.

A young college kid finally tossed some money his way. He quickly stowed it away so his cup would appear still empty. Empty empty empty. He seemed smart enough to know the tricks to get others to give up their cash for his cause. I really have no idea what his cause was. There is a good chance he had no cause. Perhaps the cause was to be able to buy the cigarettes that would probably one day kill him.

This book is not about the homeless. It is not what I thought the Mon Treal story would be about at all. I wanted to capture my love of this city...

The French. The French

Their Montreal

It really is a beautiful city with a lot of history...

You can get hot chocolate in the summer at the M Café. The M does not stand for money. It stands for magnificent. They have magnificent fine pastries. I was walking back from the café and ran into James. I had met him on the first day. Oh. He needs to be in this book. I can tell he is a really hard worker. He is a nice guy. He seems to care. I hope he always stays like that...

The Ogilvy department store of boutiques has a bagpiper walk around playing a tune every afternoon. They do that to remember their Scottish heritage. This country seems to take more pride in their heritage. Did America become such a blend that it is now only a blend and no one cares about the parts?

I watched the Montreal people one evening from my window seat at Paris Crepe on St. Catherine. Oh. My grandmother who gave me my pink rosary was named Catherine. Hi Grandma! She was the poet. I noticed that all the people wait for the walk sign before they cross the street. I wonder if they have less accidents. The hotels are pet friendly. I wonder if they love animals more than we do in the states.

Rue Crescent had a stretch of shops in houses…like the brownstones in NYC. I stopped in front of a window displaying some art. I felt like Sind…some of RL Lane's art could be in a window somewhere. Is that a sin? Their Museum of Fine Arts was decorated with sculptures that made you want to actually go inside and look around…

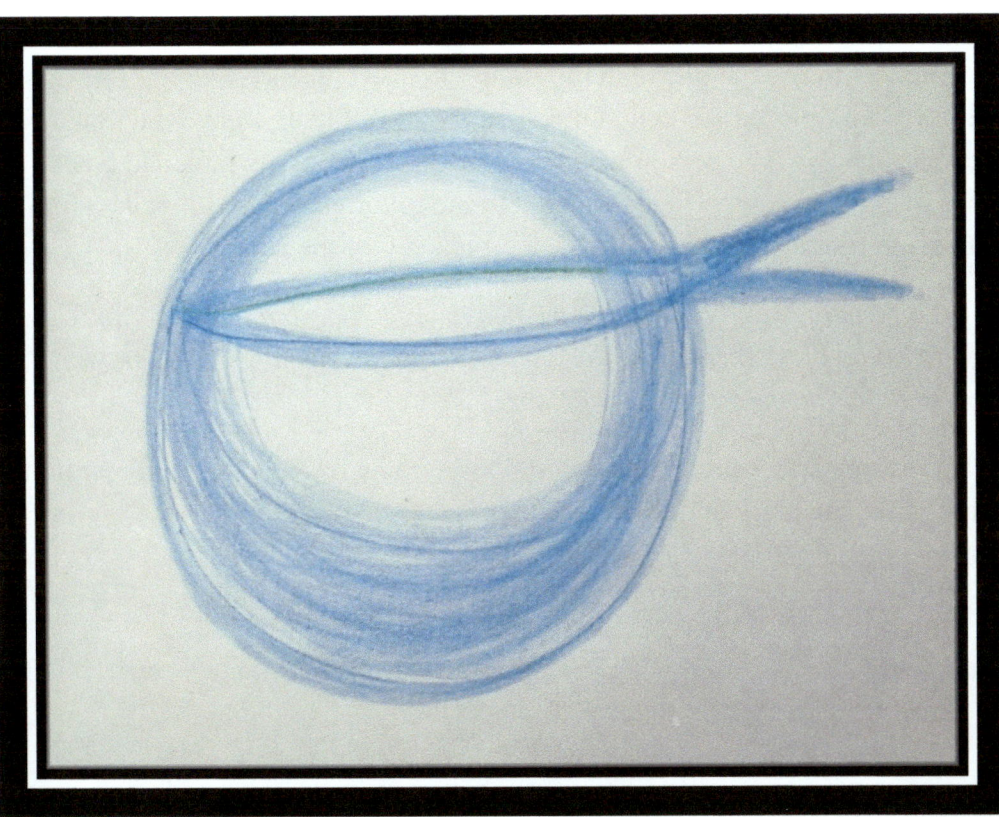

The place I stayed…Loews Hotel Vogue…it took me a few minutes to figure out how to use the phone in my room. I called for room service. They knew my name when I placed the call. Of course they would. The guy who took my order was friendly. The person who made my bed draped my pink and black rosaries over my pillow. The doorman told me to turn around as I walked into the entrance…to turn around to see the pick…pink sky of the sunset.

You can pick and choose the friends in your life…but you can't pick the strangers. Who picks them? Do the ones watching over help us with those? I am always grateful for the strangers who care.

I just realized which picture is supposed to be on the cover. I drew it during my stay. I see the mask and the flower…

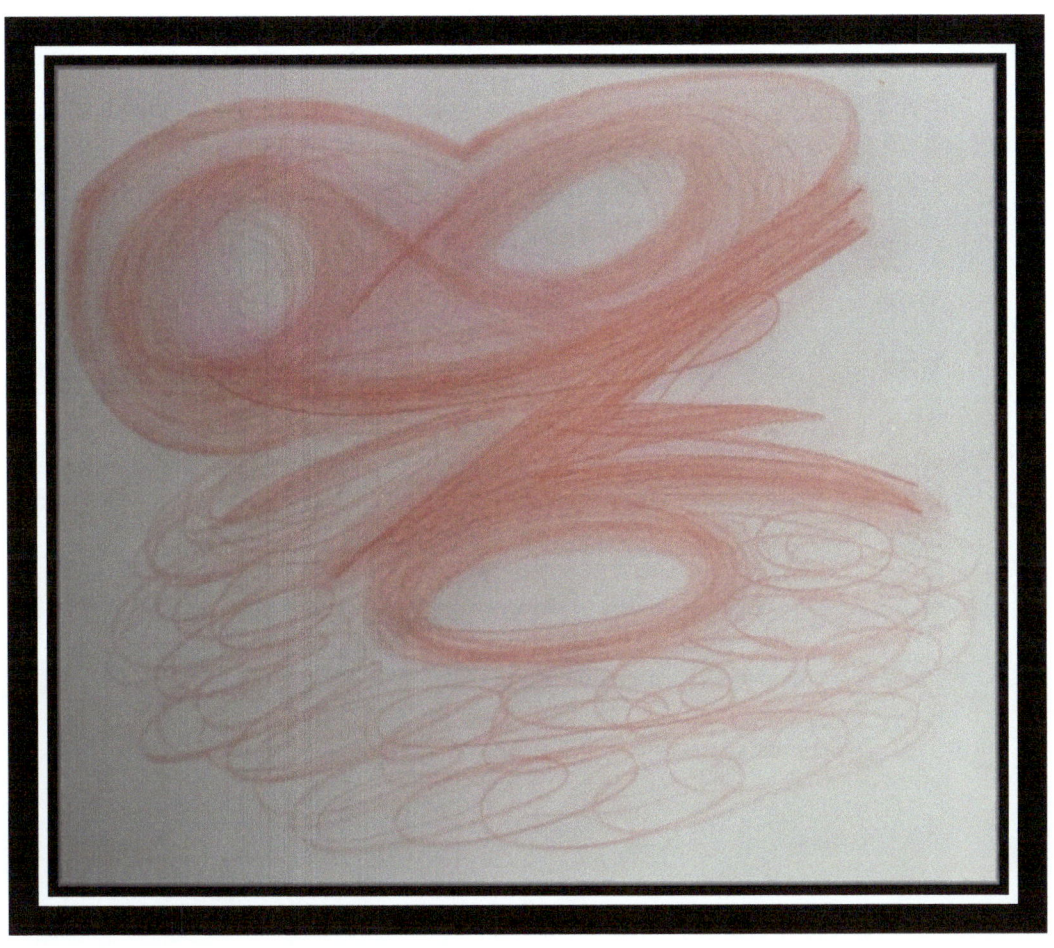

Is it a '68 or an '86? I googled Montreal and both of these years…

In 1968…

In 1968, they went to the Stanley Cup Finals against the St. Louis Blues. The Montreal Canadiens swept the series in four straight games, in the first Stanley Cup series after the NHL expansion to twelve teams. Each game was decided by only one goal

In 1986…

In 1986, they won the Stanley Cup again, but against the Calgary Flames. The Canadiens won the series four games to one making it their twenty-third Stanley Cup, and the seventeenth win out of their last eighteen Finals appearances since 1956. It was the first all-Canadian Finals since Montreal lost to the Toronto Maple Leafs in 1967, the last year of the "Original Six" era.

It makes sense. The message. They do love their team.

Oh Wait! Is it a 98? I googled Montreal and 1998…

I found the great ice storm of 1998…

Between January 4th and 10th of 1998, parts of western Quebec and other areas of Canada were hit by three successive storm fronts that have been called the greatest natural disaster in Canadian history…

The ice storm began as a low-pressure warm front from Texas and a high-pressure Arctic cold front moving in simultaneously. When the air masses collided, the warm air rose, keeping the cold air down. Snow melted at mid-level and without time to freeze coming down, it froze on the ground. There was little wind to disrupt the patterns and no sun to thaw the ice between downpours.

A state of emergency was declared…

The thickening ice downed power lines, forcing 100,000 people to seek refuge. Personnel from six Canadian provinces and eight American states worked to restore power. The Canadian Forces deployed nearly 16,000 troops in what was named "Operation Recuperation". It was the largest-ever peacetime deployment.

There was a lengthy disruption to daily life and far-reaching economic consequences. The precipitation falling as freezing rain, ice pellets and snow exceeded 100mm south of Montreal. In comparison, Canada's largest recorded ice storms, in Ottawa in 1986 and Montreal in 1961, left only 30 to 40mm of ice.

Why the story of the great ice storm? My guess is because it is a story of how the people came together for a cause. To battle the storm.

I drew the final cover that is on your book while I was in the Montreal airport waiting to return to the states. The mask and flower picture were just a part of the book I guess. I drew another plane on the return trip. I knew it had to be on the back cover. I called it "flying back"…

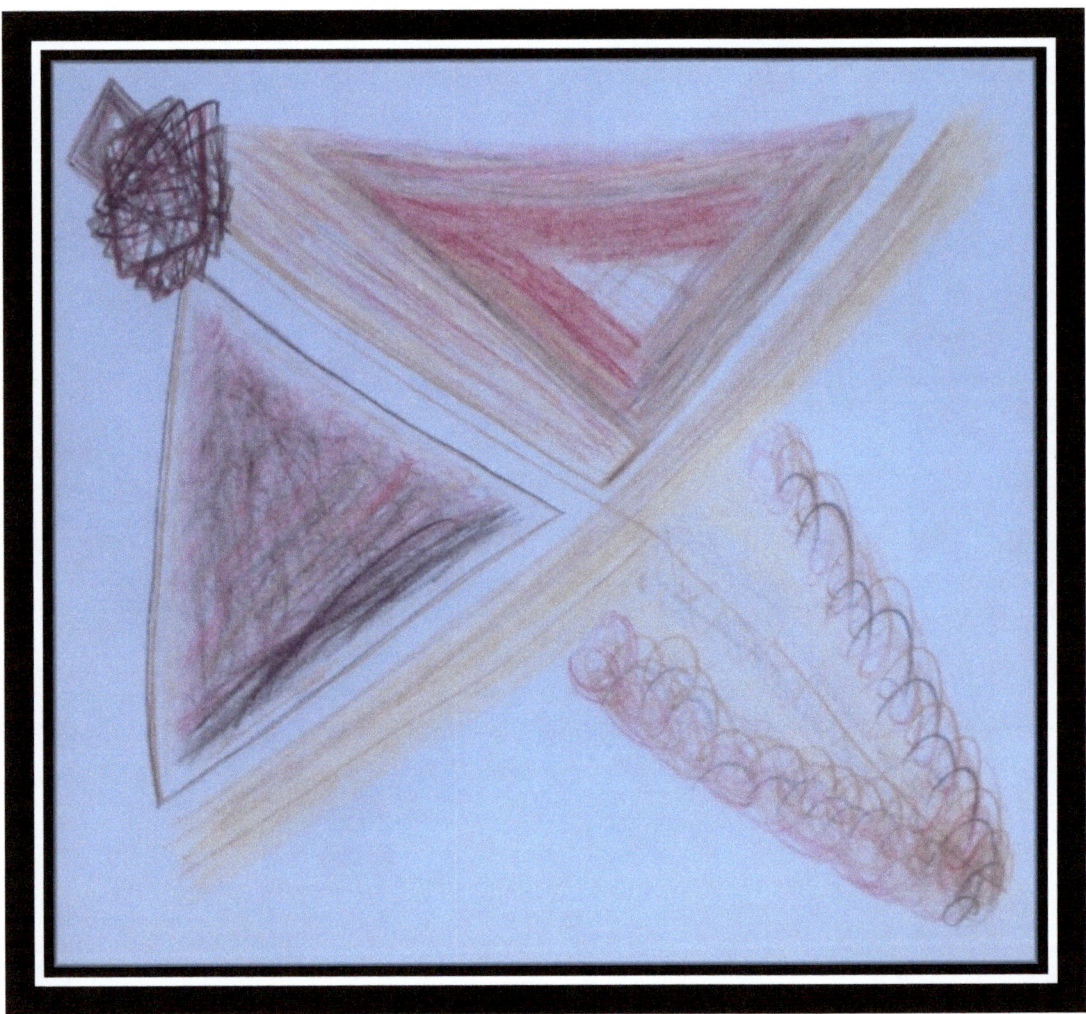

I made a new friend on that trip. Her name rhymes with pita. It is not Rita. She was pregnant…due in January. She did not know if she was having a girl or boy. I drew her picture while I was sitting next to her. I think they are saying she is having a girl…

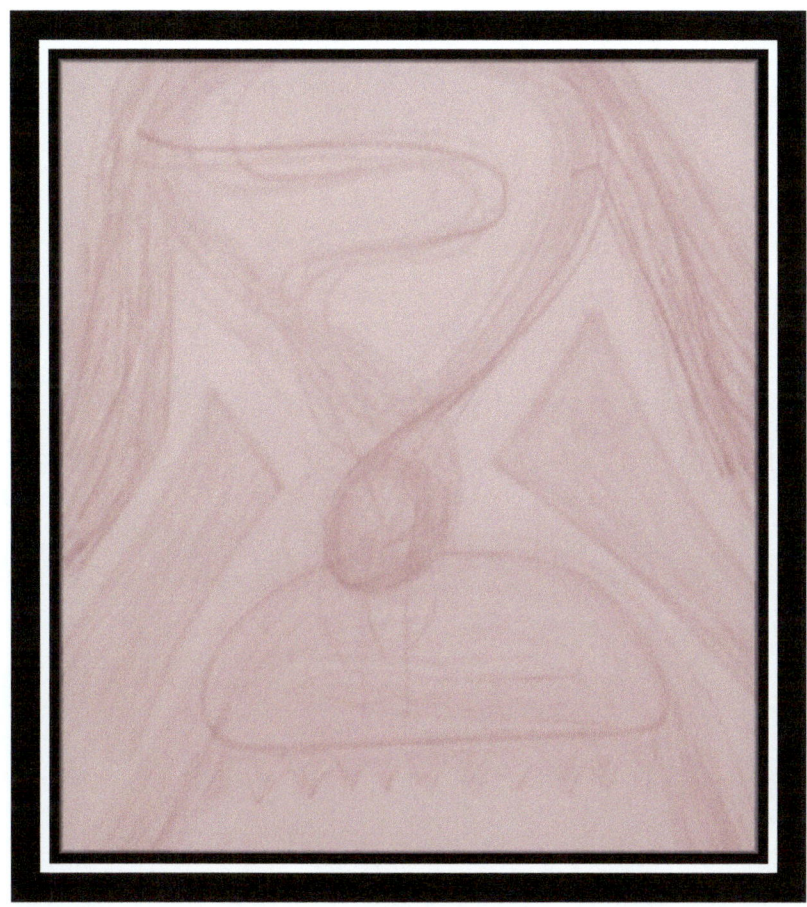

The real message of this book? I do know what it is. It is partly a message about the "other place". You have heard it before. Same people in a different place. They have the same struggles. They go to work. They question God. They look for other humans…

Montreal is, like I said from the beginning…simply Montreal.

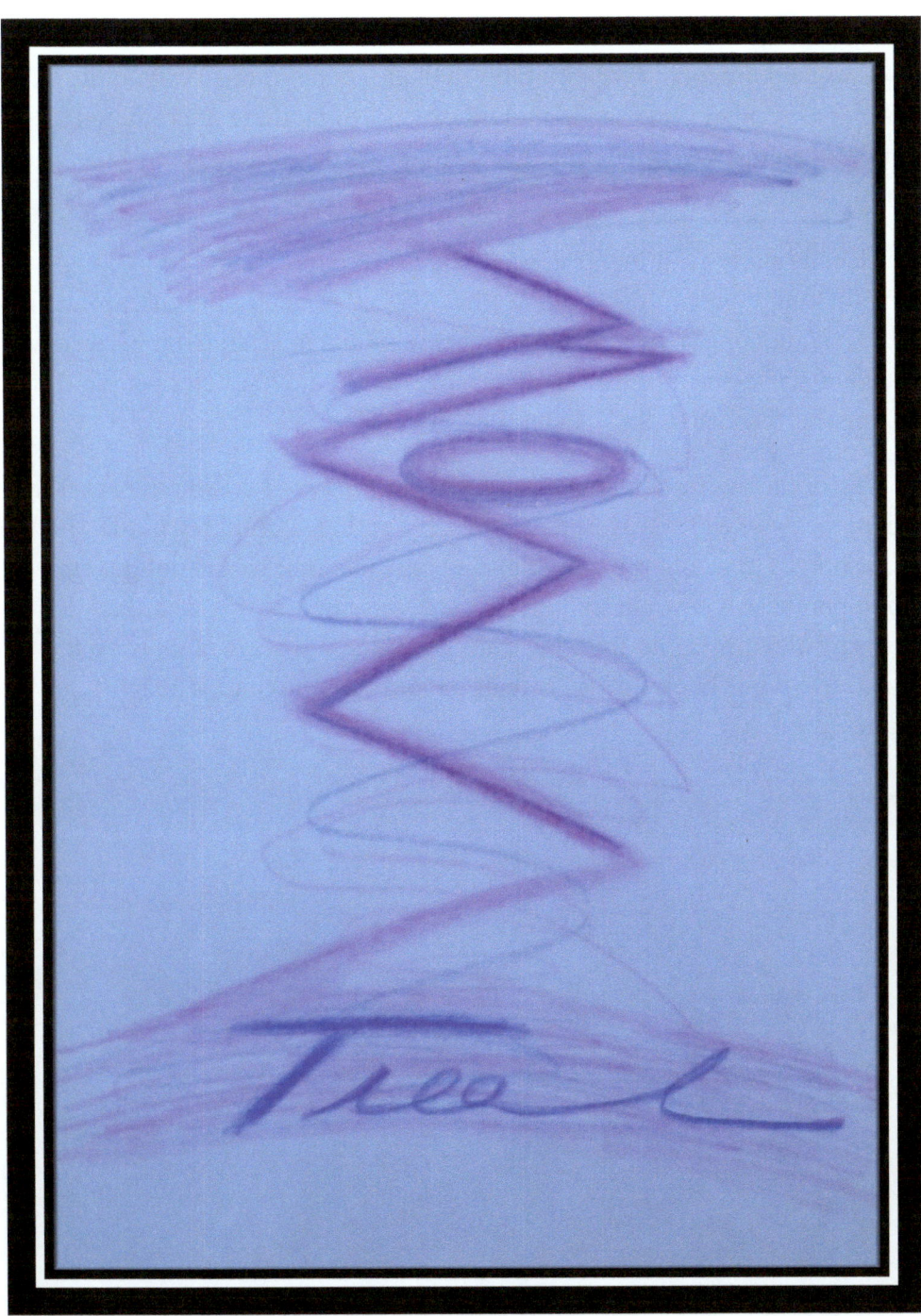

Why the homeless person? Why did he have to be in this book? Is RL Lane supposed to help him one day? Should I deliver a copy of this book to his sidewalk address? Everybody knows the homeless exist. I think there are rumors that they make more than the average middle class citizen. I think he is here for my Dad. He died from those cigarettes.

Canada started putting grotesque images of people affected by long-term smoking on their cigarette packaging. I had looked at one of the cases. The images looked like something from a horror movie that is not at all horrific because we have become so de-sensitized. They said the images did not deter people from purchasing the "cancer sticks". I can see why.

The homeless person crossed my path that day so I could remember the dependency…smoked that cigarette to the very end. He probably burned his finger it was so short. He would probably have a panic attack if he did not get enough in his cup to purchase a new pack when that one was empty. It is a hard addiction to quick. I saw a lot of people smoking during my stay. It seemed more so than back in the states. So this book I guess is really about the smoking. The RL Lane way to tell you to quit…

Q – Quickly. Do it now...

U – Under the pillow. Look under your pillow at the rosary that should be there. Ask him to help you...

I – I don't have a creative way to tell you...

T – *Today is the day you should quit.*

"I knew for a long time that the smoking story would make its way to the pages. I was actually surprised that it came out in the Montreal Story. Why Dad? Oh. I guess he did like his French-Canadian in-laws even if they were not that fond of him..." RL Lane.

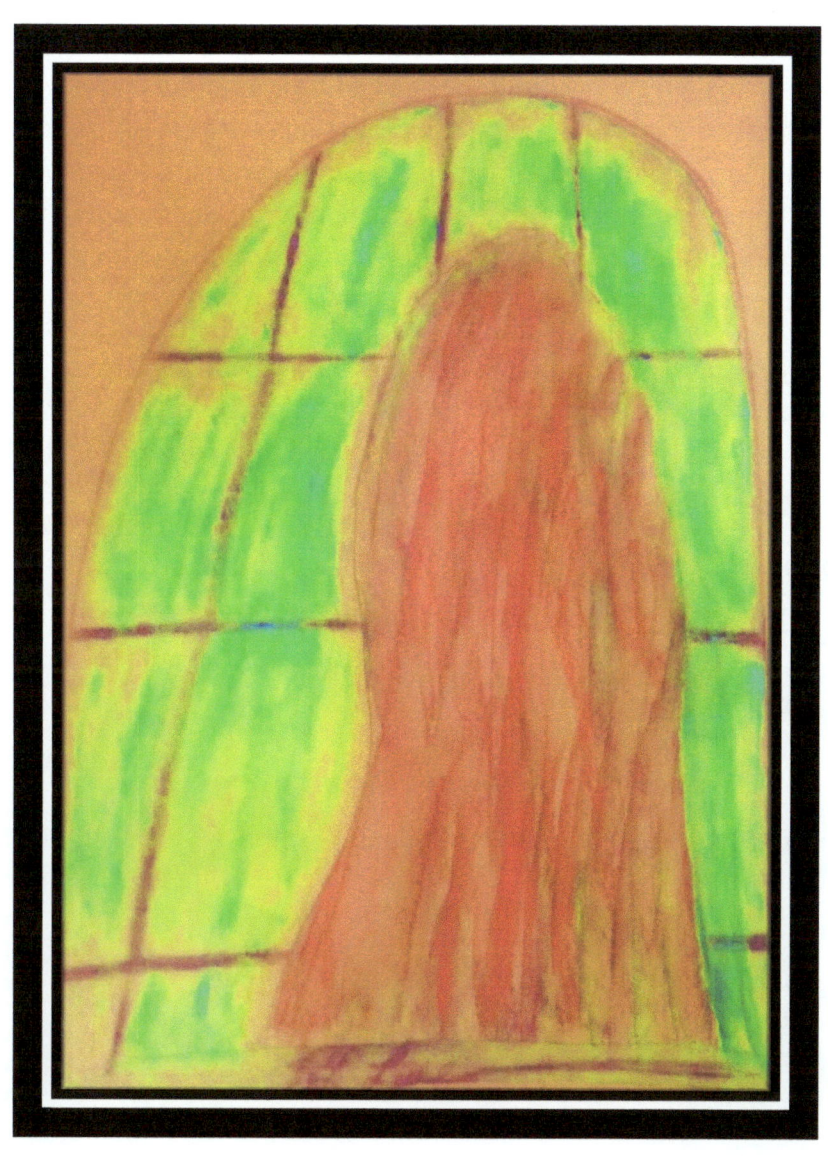

In loving memory of

Joseph W. Vogt

Somewhere along the pages of EcarreT, I had talked about my Dad's smoking. His years cut short. I told the story of how as an adult, I never told him to quit. I certainly did not want him to die from the long-term effects of smoking. I somehow felt it made him lesser of a man for me, his child, to tell him to quit. It is true though. Sometimes our children are wiser, smerter...smarter, stronger. I am no subject matter expert on a lot of things, but I can tell you it is ok to take advice from your children sometimes.

"Are you sure you're going to be happy in the city?" she asked me. I thought about it. My daughter is very perceptive. I doubt it is the best place for me, but it is most likely only short-term. I just need to go there. For RL Lane and I need to go now...

Go now...

Quit now...

Or I may never go...

Or you may never quit...

Or I may never get the chance to live in the city...

Or you may never get the chance to quit smoking...

Or I may never get the chance to become RL Lane...

Or you may never get the chance to quit the bad marriage...

Or we may never get the chance...

I was in Montreal on July 20-22 of 2015. Oh. It is still the year 2015. It'll make me sad when these words remain after I am gone…

...Treal. My treal. My tree. My tree all. All my tree. All my trees. It is true, my Dad loved to see all the trees...

Who are Thad and Lillie? Well I guess they are the tadpole and lily pad. Memories from my Mom and her summer days at the family camp. I feel like those are supposed to be character names or something in the future…perhaps just a book title…

"Thad and Lillie"

About the Author and *Illustrator*

RL Lane has published the EcarreT series and a collection of short story art books featuring the author's illustrations. The EcarreT series begins with "Chapel Street Signs"…

…unexplained connections that challenge us to beli ve. A woman, a Dad a Doctor, a cat and mouse, a horse and tale tell their stories. "Do you beli ve in spirits?" I asked my friend. "Well look", he said, "I believe there are things that cannot be explained…" Oh. Plus, hear ov a Mom's battle with her struggle to connect to the woman…her little girl.

Welcome to EcarreT…a world
Where everyone cares
Why did I have to create it in…

A fiction fantasy world?

You may already know why, but you will see regardless of what you believe as a girl's journey of love and faith on her "Touring Machine" take her on the best journey of her mundane life. A life well on its way takes a turn in a direction that could've never been seen or even dreamed…

The author can be contacted at:

RosaLeeeLane@gmail.com
www.Amazon.com/author/readrllane

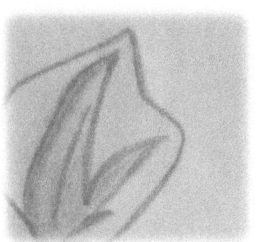

www.ingramcontent.com/pod-product-compliance
Lightning Source LLC
Chambersburg PA
CBHW050908180526
45159CB00007B/2832